A NIGHT WITH janis joplin

T0065959

ISBN 978-1-4803-6855-2

HAL•LEONARD®
CORPORATION

7777 W. BLUEMOUND RD. P.O. BOX 13819 MILWAUKEE, WI 53213

www.janisjoplin.com

Visit Hal Leonard Online at
www.halleonard.com

Daniel Chilewich   Todd Gershwin   Michael Cohl

Jeffrey Jampol   Red Tail Entertainment   Stephen Tenenbaum   Michael J. Moritz Jr./Brunish & Trinchero

Richard Winkler   Ginger Productions   Bill Ham   Claudio Loureiro   Keith Mardak

Ragovoy Entertainment   Bob & Laurie Wolfe/Neil Kahanovitz   Jerry Rosenberg/AJ Michaels   Mike Stoller & Corky Hale Stoller

Darren P. DeVerna   Susan DuBow   Tanya Grubich   Jeremiah H. Harris   Herb Spivak

PRESENT

Presented in association with The Estate of Janis Joplin and Jeffrey Jampol for JAM, Inc.

STARRING

Mary Bridget Davies

Taprena Michelle Augustine   De'Adre Aziza   Nikki Kimbrough   NaTasha Yvette Williams

Allison Blackwell   Alison Cusano

AND

Kacee Clanton

SCENIC & LIGHTING DESIGN	COSTUME DESIGN	SOUND DESIGN	PROJECTION DESIGN
Justin Townsend	Amy Clark	Carl Casella	Darrel Maloney

HAIR & MAKE-UP DESIGN	CREATIVE CONSULTANT	CASTING
Leah J. Loukas	Red Awning/Jack Viertel	Laura Stanczyk Casting

PRODUCTION MANAGER	PRESS REPRESENTATIVE	ADVERTISING & MARKETING
Hudson Theatrical Associates	Boneau Bryan-Brown	twenty6two/AKA

GENERAL MANAGER	PRODUCTION STAGE MANAGER	EXECUTIVE PRODUCER
Bespoke Theatricals	J. Philip Bassett	Red Awning

MUSIC DIRECTOR & CONDUCTOR	ORIGINAL MUSIC ARRANGER & DIRECTOR	MUSIC COORDINATOR
Ross Seligman	Len Rhodes	Howard Joines

CHOREOGRAPHY BY

Patricia Wilcox

WRITTEN AND DIRECTED BY

Randy Johnson

Produced in 2012 by Arena Stage
Molly Smith, Artistic Director   Edgar Dobie, Executive Director

Produced in 2012 by Cleveland Play House
Michael Bloom, Artistic Director   Kevin Moore, Managing Director

The Producers wish to express their appreciation to Theatre Development Fund for its support of this production.

Opening Night: October 10, 2013

TELL MAMA

Words and Music by CLARENCE CARTER,
MARCUS DANIEL and WILBUR TERRELL

You thought you had __ to find __ a good girl,

one to love you and give you the world.

Now you find __ that

you've been mis-used. Talk to me, _____ I'll do what you choose. _ I want _ you to

tell Ma - ma all a-bout _ it; tell Ma-

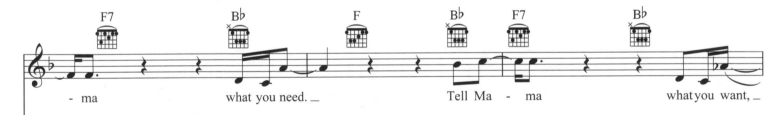

- ma what you need. _ Tell Ma - ma what you want, _

To Coda ⊕

and I'll make ev-'ry-thing all right. __

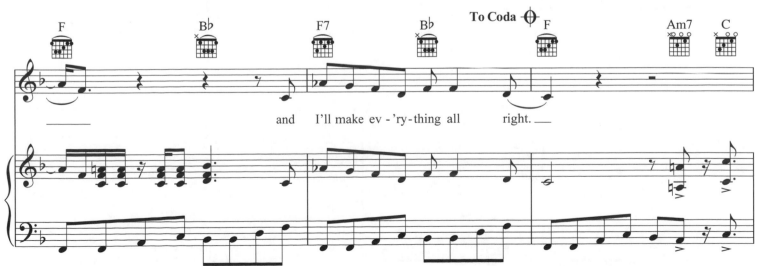

That girl you had __ did-n't have no sense. She was - n't worth all the

time that you spent. She had oth - er man ___ throw you out-doors.

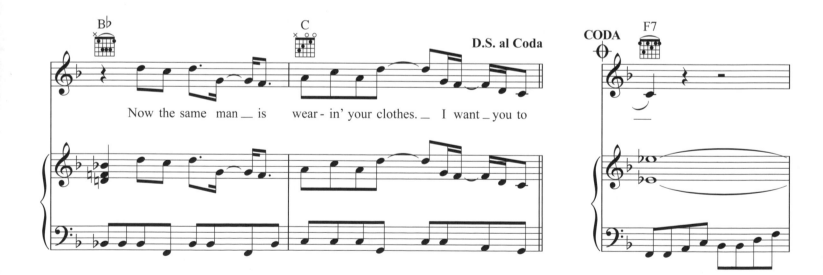

D.S. al Coda

CODA

Now the same man __ is wear-in' your clothes. __ I want __ you to

She would em-bar - rass you an - y where. She let ev-'ry - bod - y know

she did-n't care. Give me a chance, _ I've been beg - gin' you.

I just wan-na take care ___ of you. _____ I want _ you to tell Ma-

MAYBE

Words and Music by
RICHARD BARRETT

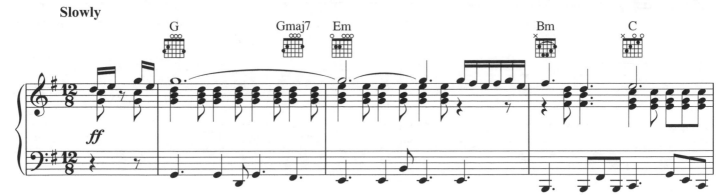

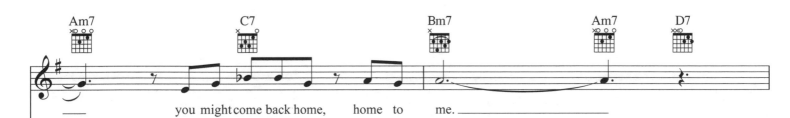

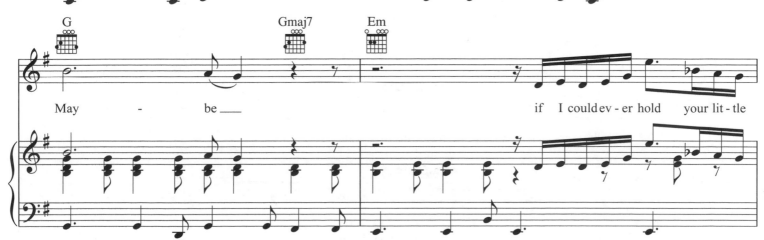

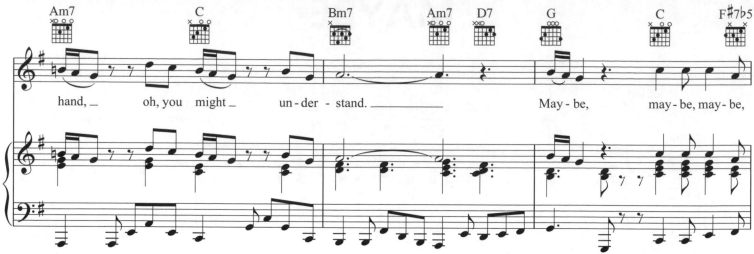

Please, _ please, _ please, _ please, oh, won't you re-con-sid-er, ba-by. Now come on. I said,

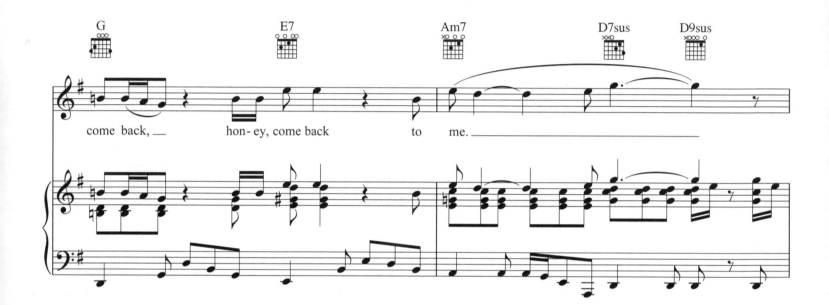

come back, _ hon-ey, come back to me. _____

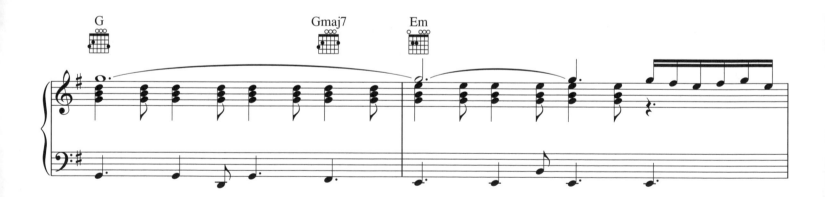

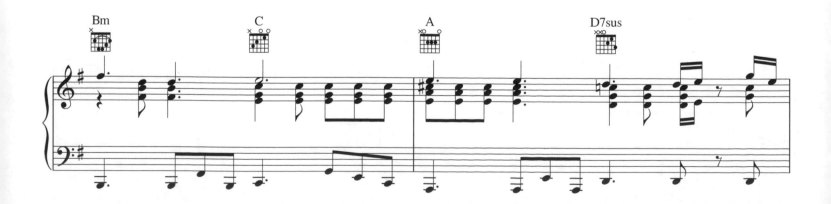

SUMMERTIME
from PORGY AND BESS®

Music and Lyrics by GEORGE GERSHWIN,
DuBOSE and DOROTHY HEYWARD and IRA GERSHWIN

Moderately slow

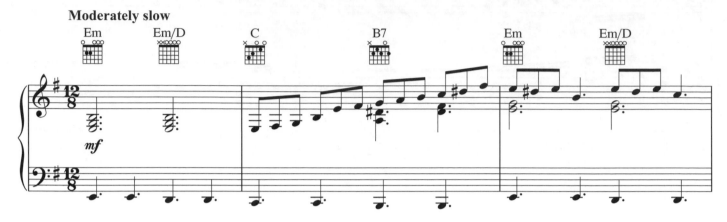

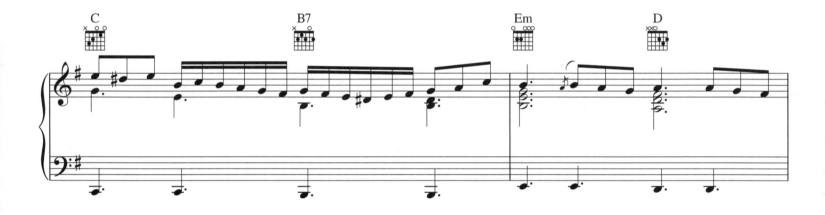

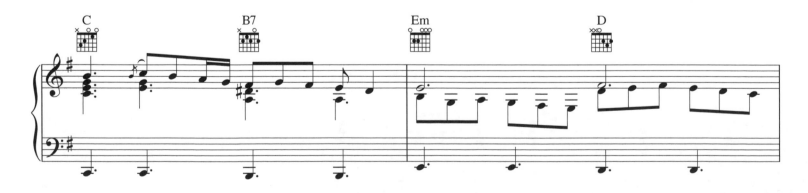

don't you cry. _____

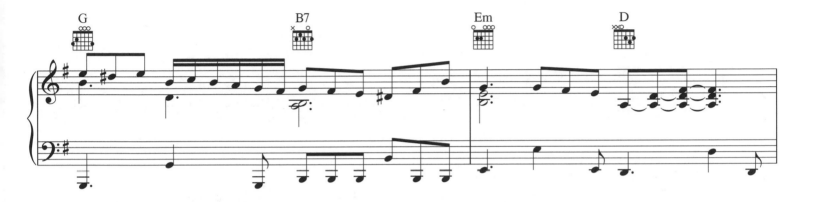

D.S. al Coda

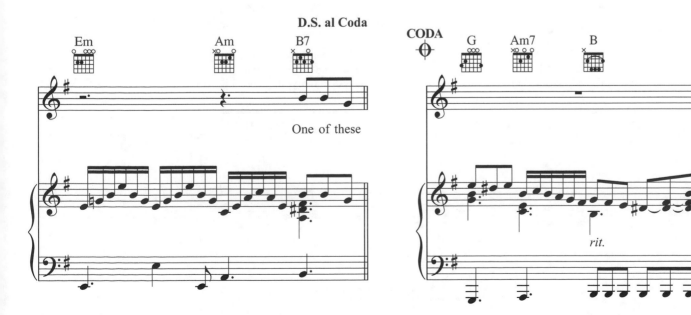

One of these

CODA

TURTLE BLUES

Words and Music by
JANIS JOPLIN

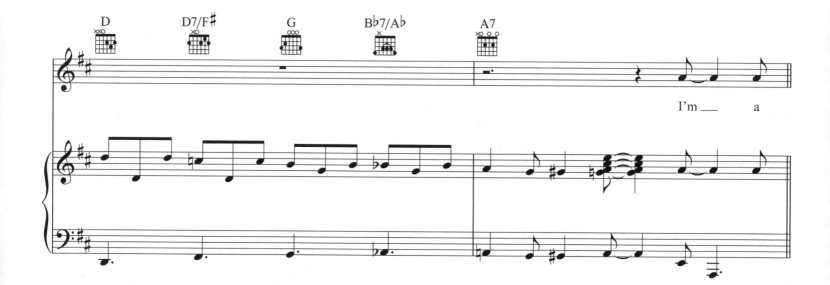

I'm ___ a

mean, _____ mean wom-an, _____
once _____ had a dad-dy, _____
ain't the kind of wom-an _____

I don't need no one man, _____ no
He said he'd give me ev-'ry-thing in
who'd make your life a bed _____ of

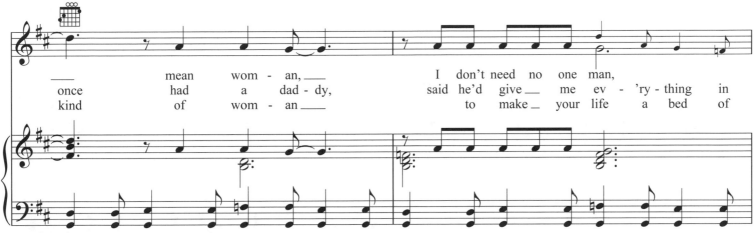

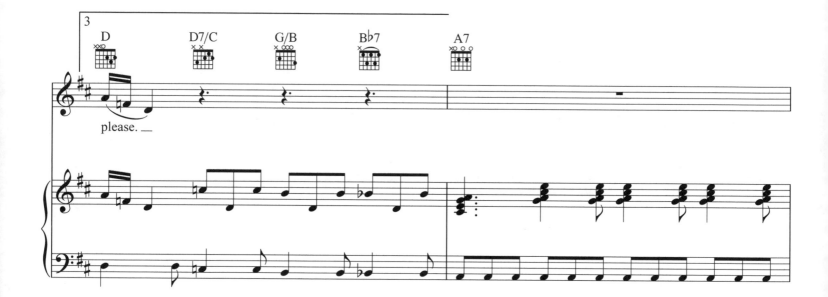

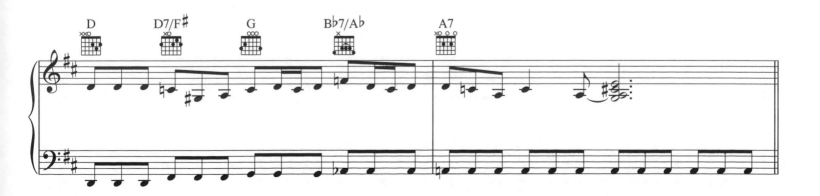

I guess I'm just like a tur - tle, _____ that's hid-in' un - der-neath its hard-ened

shell. Whoa, _ whoa, _____ whoa, oh,

yeah, _ like a tur - tle, ___ hid-in' un - der-neath its hard-ened

shell. But you

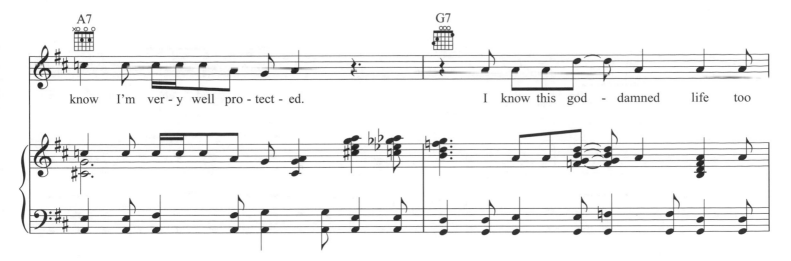

know I'm ver-y well pro-tect-ed.   I know this god-damned life too

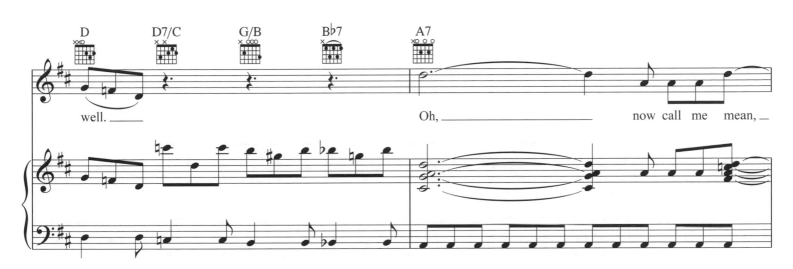

well. _____   Oh, _____ now call me mean, _

_____ you can call me e-vil, _____ yeah, yeah,   I've been called much worse things a-

round.   Call me

24

mean   or call me e - vil, _____   I've been called much worse things   a -

round.   Yeah, but

I'm gon-na take good care of Jan - is,   yeah,   hon-ey, no one gon-na dog   me

down. _

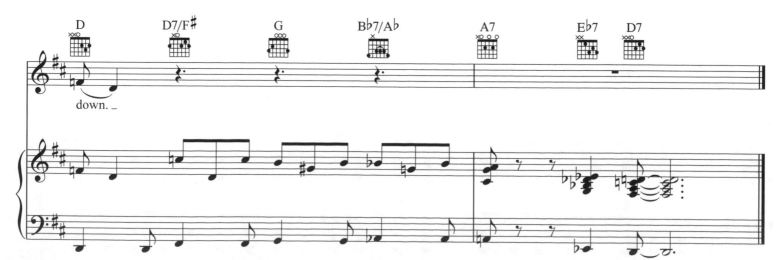

DOWN ON ME

Words and Music by
JANIS JOPLIN

Fast Rock

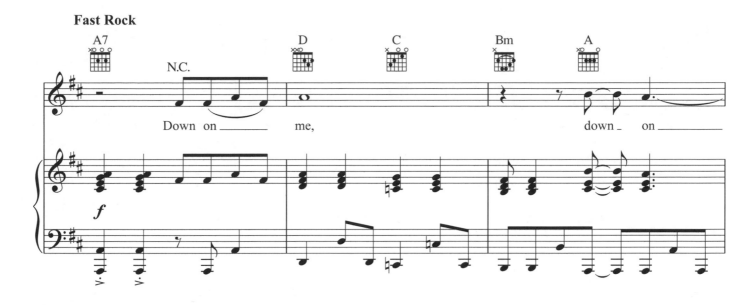

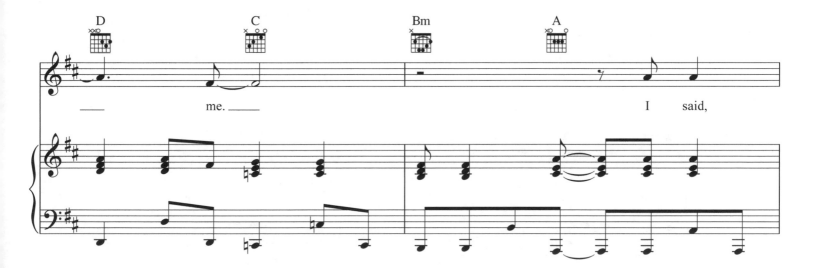

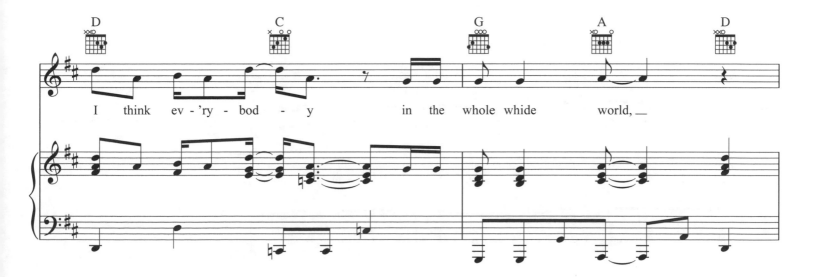

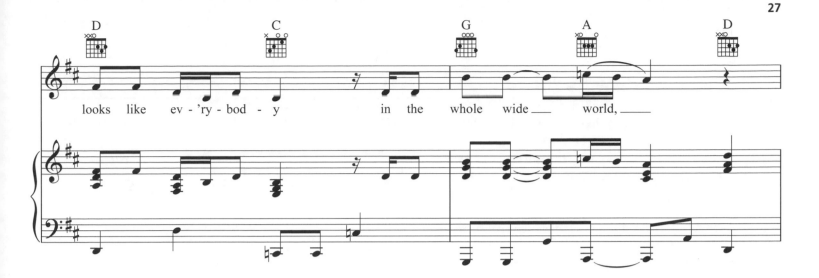

looks like ev-'ry-bod - y in the whole wide ___ world, ___

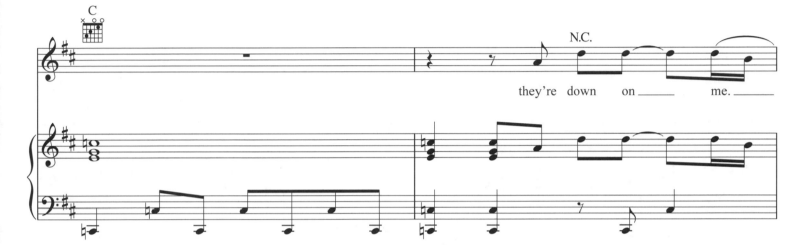

they're down on ___ me. ___

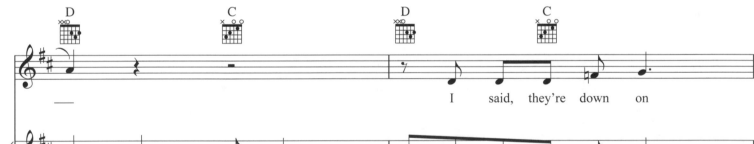

I said, they're down on

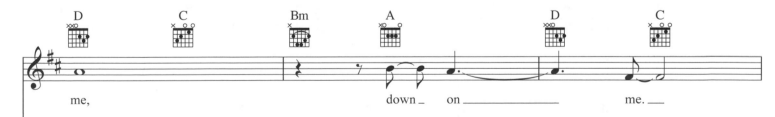

me, down ___ on ___ me. ___

Oh, ___ and I said, it looks like ev - 'ry - bod - y ___ in the

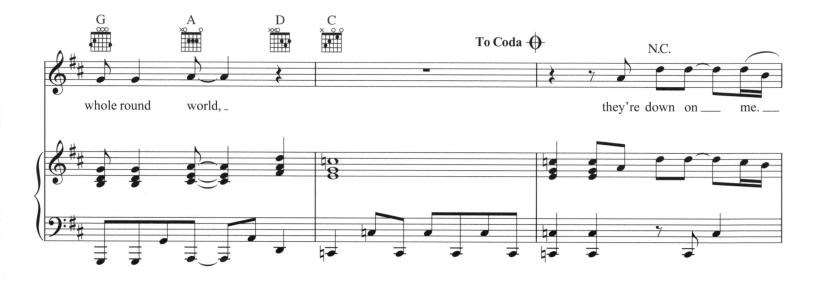

whole round world, ___   they're down on ___ me. ___

Guitar solo

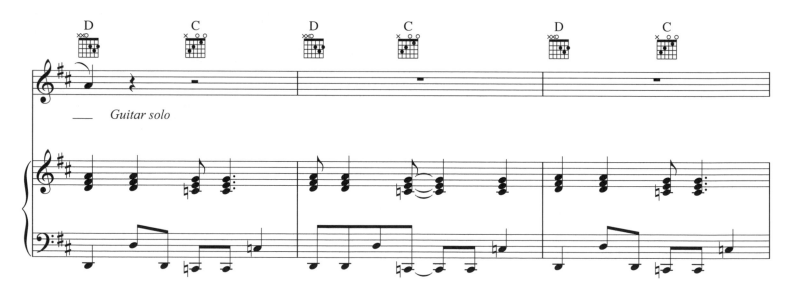

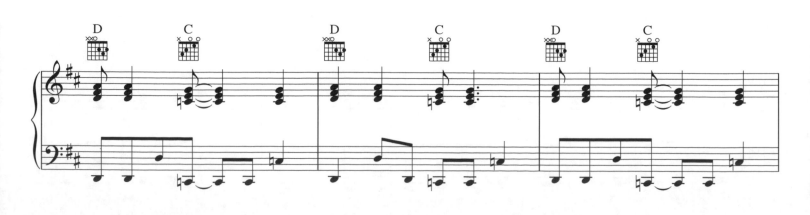

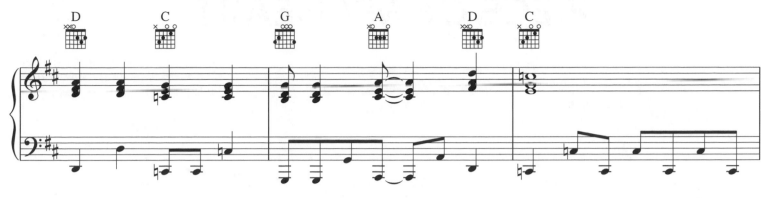

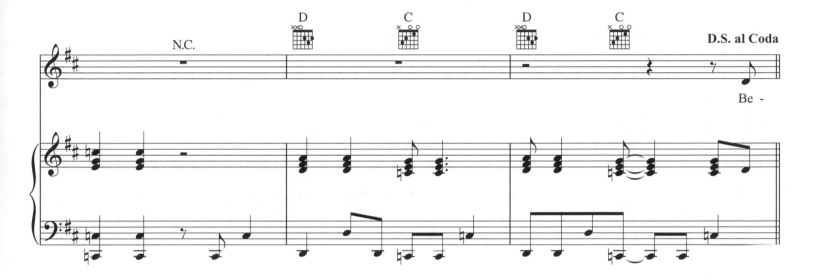

D.S. al Coda

Be -

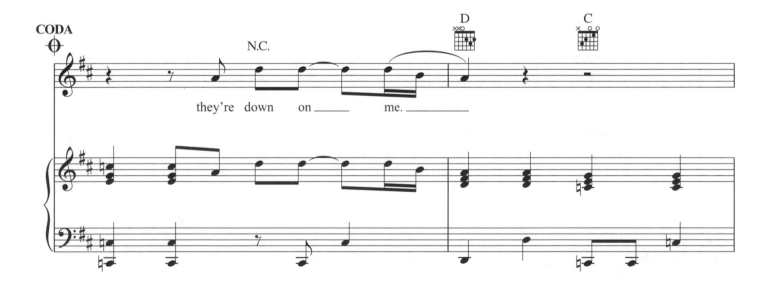

CODA

they're down on _____ me. _____

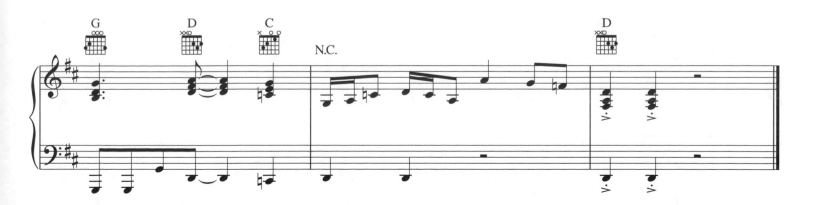

PIECE OF MY HEART

Words and Music by BERT BERNS
and JERRY RAGOVOY

Driving Rock

Ooh come _ on, come _ on, come _ on, come _ on.

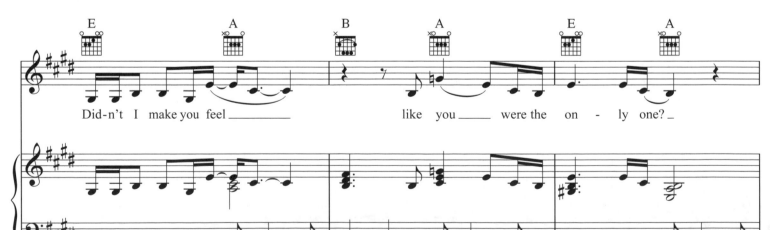

Did-n't I make you feel _____ like you _____ were the on - ly one? _

Yeah, __ said did-n't I give ya near-ly ev-'ry-thing that a wom-an

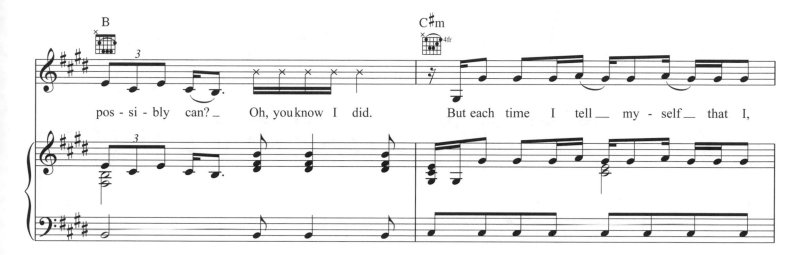

pos-si-bly can? __ Oh, you know I did. But each time I tell __ my-self __ that I,

I think I've had e-nough, __ oh, __ I'm _____ gon-na show _ you, ba-by, a

wom-an can _ be tough. __ I want you to come _ on, come _ on, come _ on, come _ on and

34

I can't stand the pain, __ you take me in __ your arms __ and I'm

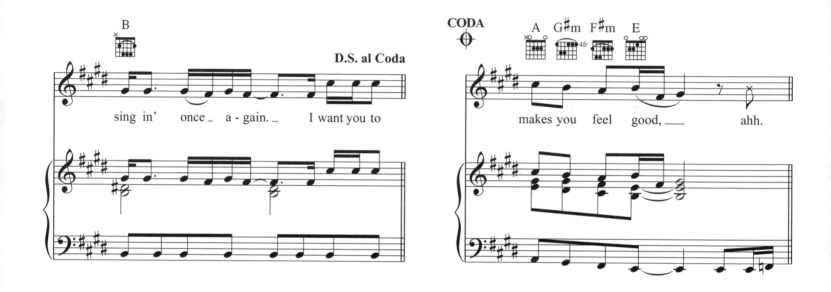

sing in' once __ a - gain. __ I want you to

CODA

makes you feel good, __ ahh.

D.S. al Coda

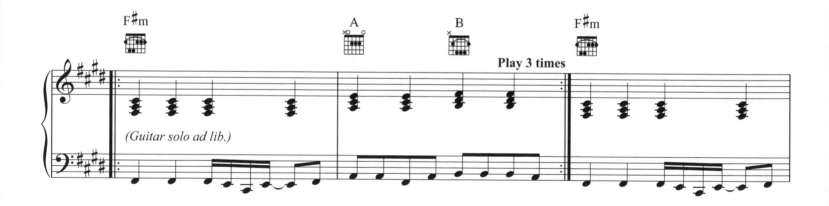

(Guitar solo ad lib.)

Play 3 times

(End solo)

Come ____ on, come ____ on, come ____ on, come ____ on and

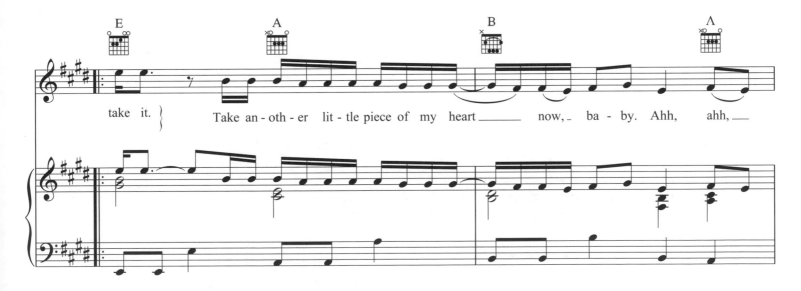

take it. } Take an - oth - er lit - tle piece of my heart ____ now, _ ba - by. Ahh, ahh, ___

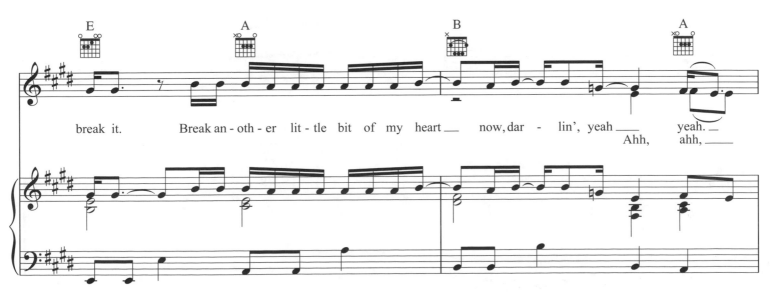

break it. Break an - oth - er lit - tle bit of my heart ____ now, dar - lin', yeah ____ yeah. ___
Ahh, ahh, ____

have a,   have an-oth-er lit-tle piece of my heart ___ now, _ ba - by. ___

1

You know you've got ___ it,   whaa. _____

2

You know you've got ___ it,   child, if it makes you feel good. ___

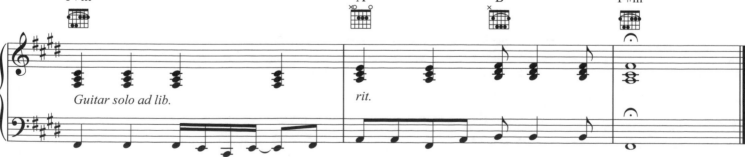

Guitar solo ad lib.   *rit.*

TODAY I SING THE BLUES

Words and Music by
CURTIS LEWIS

Slow Blues

N.C.

Spoken: "What is this thing called the blues? It's called time."

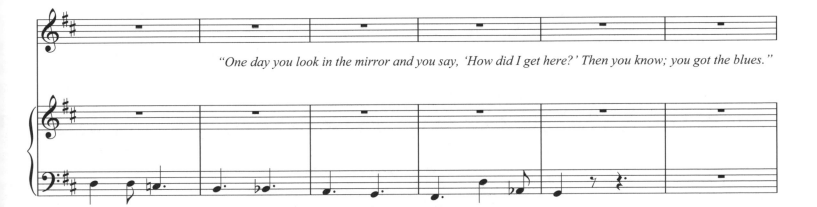

"One day you look in the mirror and you say, 'How did I get here?' Then you know; you got the blues."

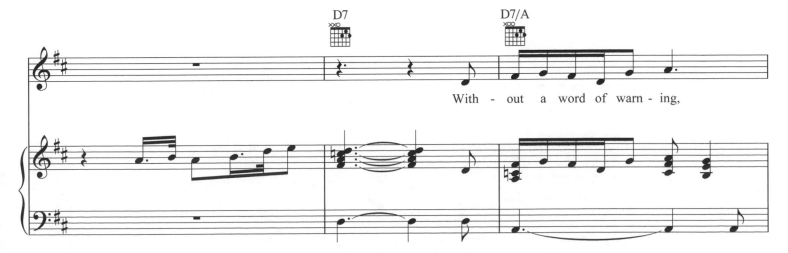

D7   D7/A

With - out a word of warn - ing,

the blues _____ walked in this morn - ing

and cir - cled 'round ____   My lone - ly room. _____   I did - n't know

why   I had this sad and lone - ly feel - ing

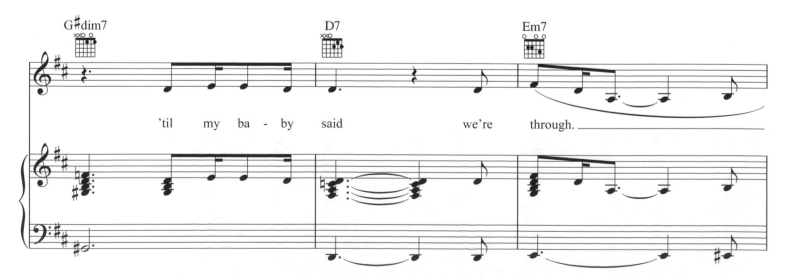

'til my ba - by said   we're   through. _____

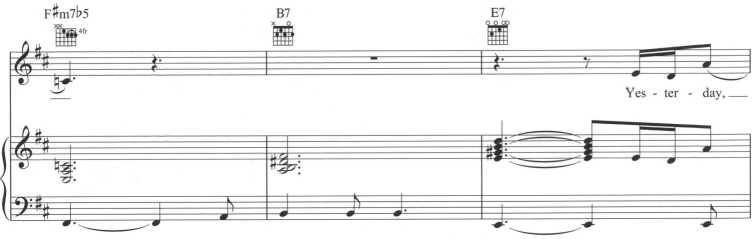

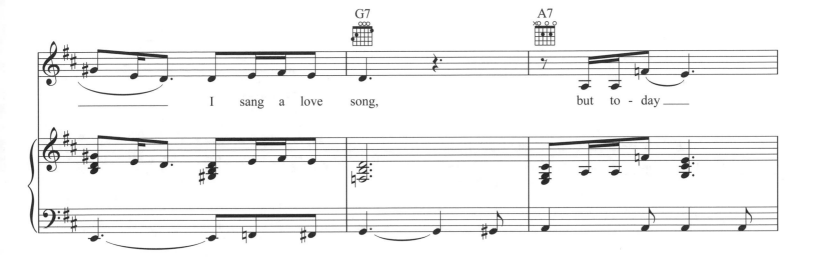

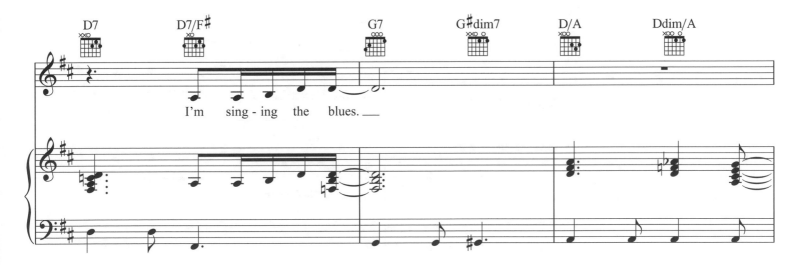

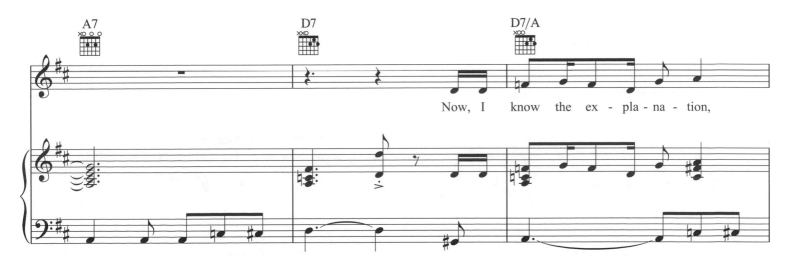

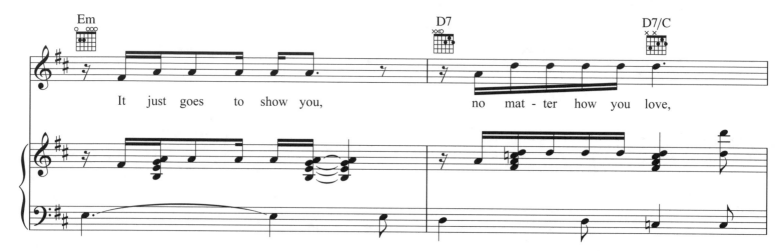

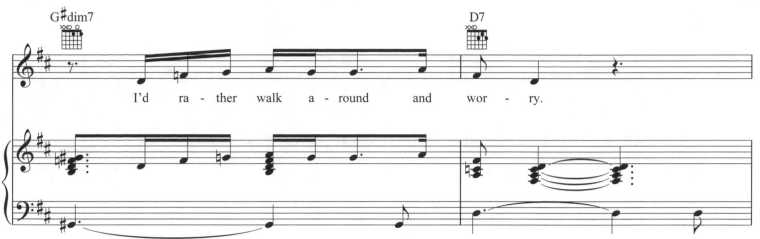

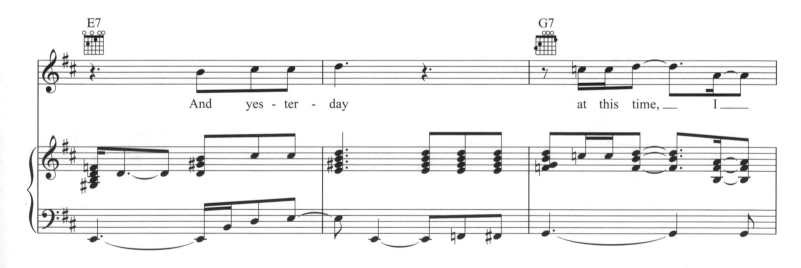

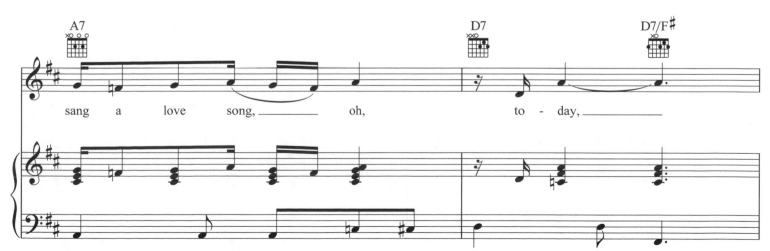

my sto-ry's a lit-tle dif-f'rent, peo-ple, do you hear me, I'm sing-ing the blues. _____ Yeah, yeah,

yeah, yeah, _ yeah. _____ Now, _ it strikes me kind of fun-ny

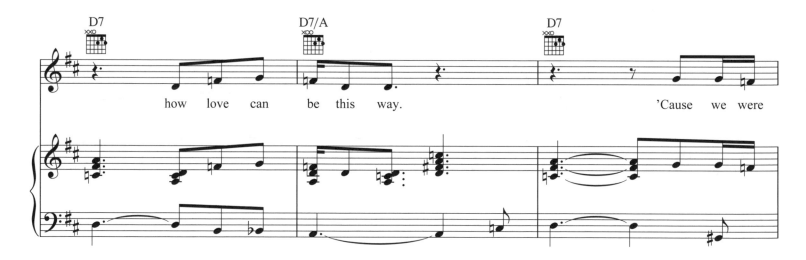

how love can be this way. _____ 'Cause we were

lov-ers last _ night, hon-ey, _____ oh, but I'm sit-ting a-lone a-gain, _

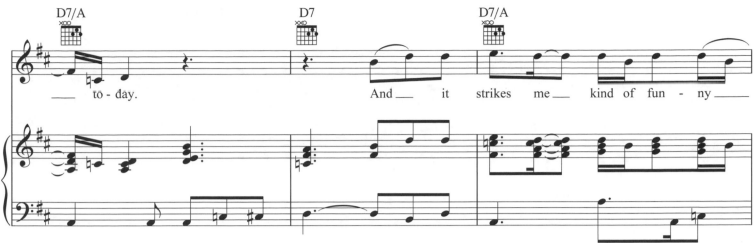

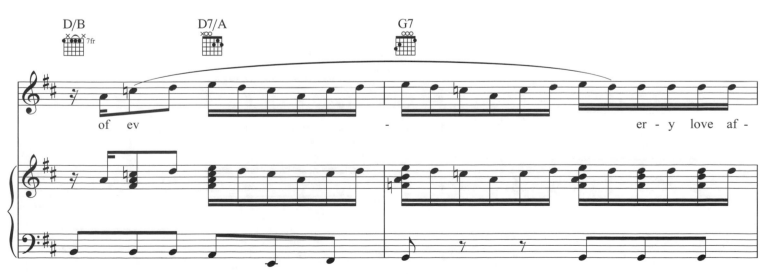

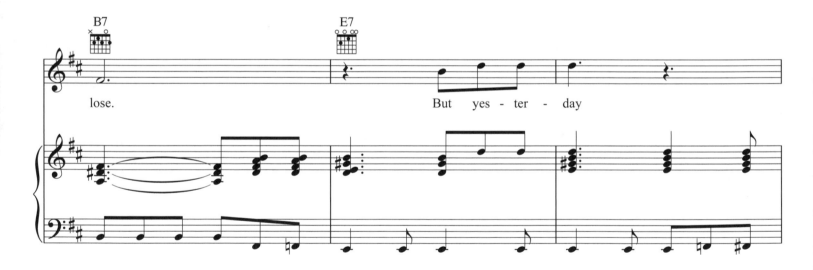

but right now,   but right now,   oh, _____

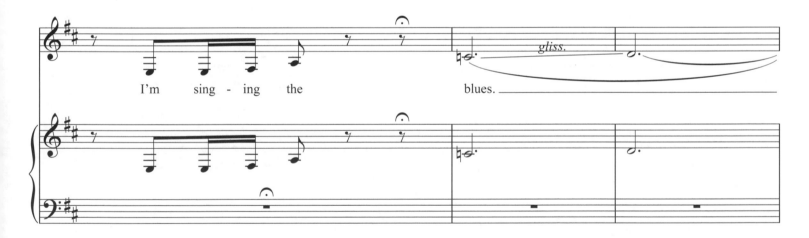

I'm sing - ing the   blues. _____

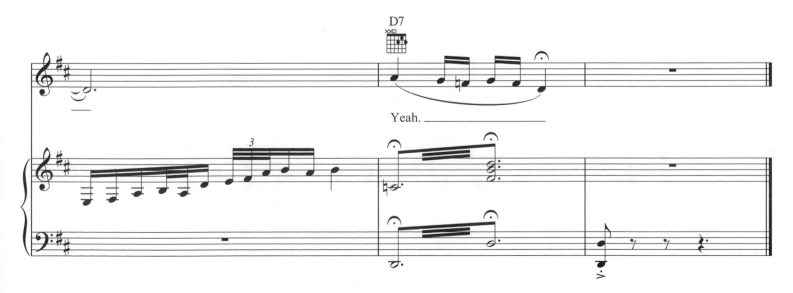

Yeah. _____

NOBODY KNOWS YOU WHEN YOU'RE DOWN AND OUT

Words and Music by
JIMMIE COX

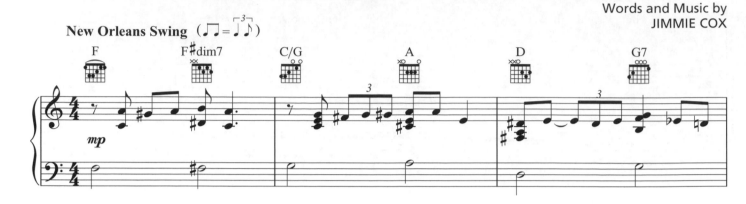

Once I ___ lived the life of a mil - lio - naire.

Spent all my ___ mon-ey, I did-n't care   Car-ry-ing my friends out

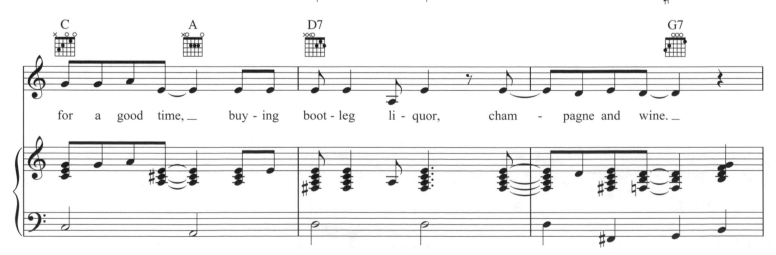

for a good time, ___ buy-ing boot-leg li-quor, cham-pagne and wine. ___

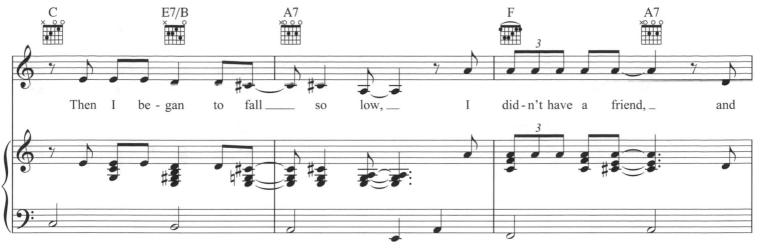

Then I be-gan to fall so low, I did-n't have a friend, and

no place to go. But if I ev-er get my hands on a dol-lar a-gain, I'm gon-na

hold on to it 'til them ea-gles grin. No - bod-y knows you

when you're down and out. In my pock-et, not one pen - ny.

And my friends, I have-n't an-y. But if I ev-er get on my_

_ feet a - gain, _ then I'll_ meet my long lost friend. _

It's not as strange with-out a doubt, _ no-bod-y knows you when you're

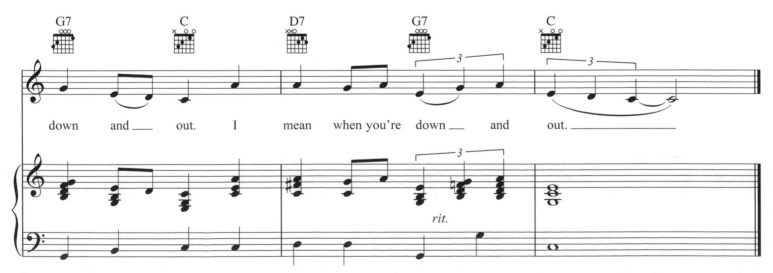

down and _ out. I mean when you're down _ and out. _____

SPIRIT IN THE DARK

Words and Music by
ARETHA FRANKLIN

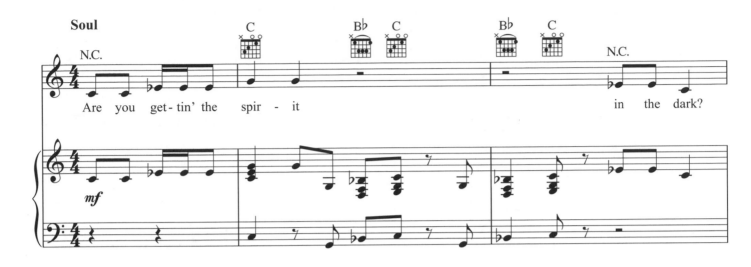

Are you get-tin' the spir - it in the dark?

Are you get-tin' the spir - it _____

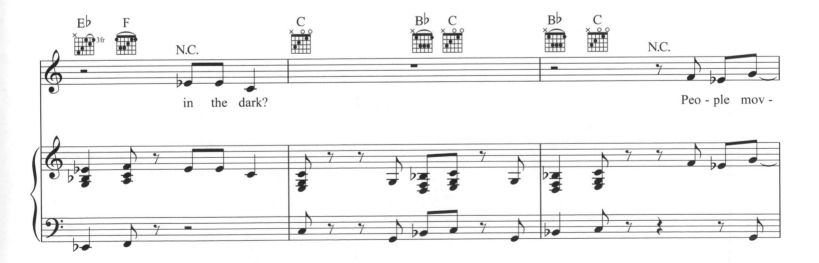

in the dark? Peo - ple mov-

-in'. Hey, ain't __ we groov - in'? _____

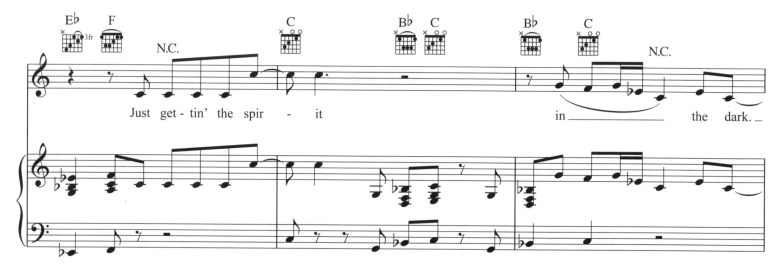

Just get - tin' the spir - it in _____ the dark. __

Tell me sis - ter,

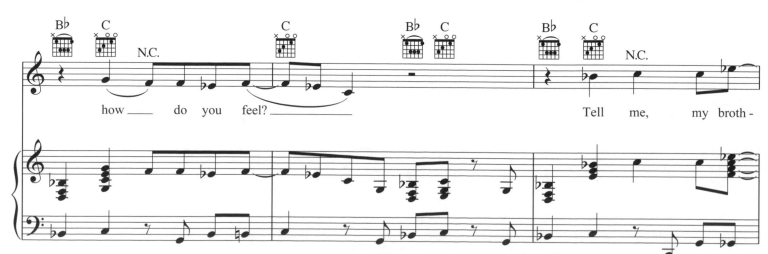

how __ do you feel? _____ Tell me, my broth -

It's like Sal - ly Walk - er,   sit - tin'   in   a   sauc -

- er.   That's   how   we   do   it   now. __

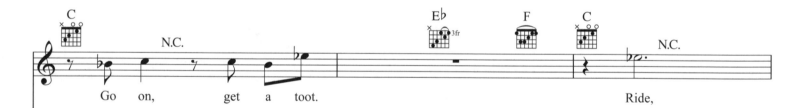

Go   on,   get   a   toot.   Ride,

Sal - ly,   ride, __ oh, put your hands on your hips, __ girl, and cov - er your eyes. __ Come on and

it.

Call my broth-er,   call my

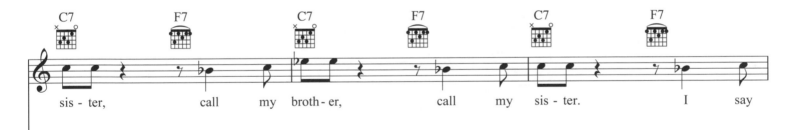

sis-ter,   call my broth-er,   call my sis-ter.   I say

yeah,   (yeah)   yeah,   (yeah)   yeah yeah,   (yeah yeah)

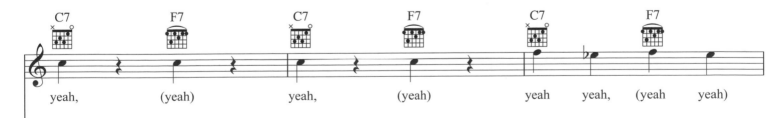

yeah   yeah, (yeah   yeah)   yeah yeah yeah yeah yeah yeah yeah yeah   yeah yeah yeah yeah yeah yeah yeah yeah

yeah yeah yeah yeah yeah yeah yeah yeah.   Oh,   feel   the   spir - it,   (ooh)

yeah,   (ooh)   yeah, _____ (ooh)   yeah yeah yeah (ooh)

yeah,   (ooh)   yeah!

TRY
(Just A Little Bit Harder)

Words and Music by JERRY RAGOVOY
and CHIP TAYLOR

Moderately, with a beat

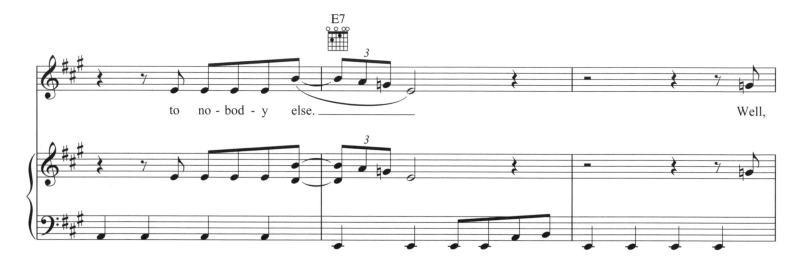

just a lit-tle bit hard - er so I won't lose, lose, lose ____ you

to no-bod-y else. ____ Well,

I don't care ____ how long it's gon-na take me, but if it's a dream ___ I don't want, ___

(Spoken):
____ No, I don't really want it. If it's a dream ___ I don't want ____ no-bod-y to

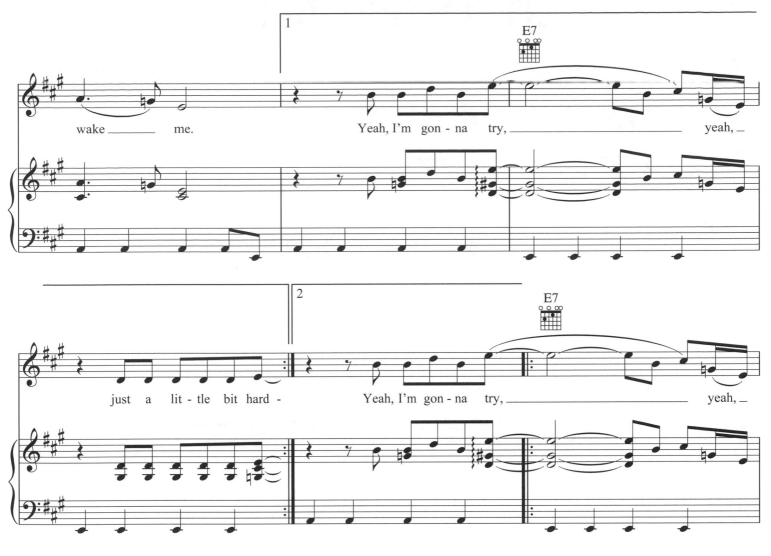

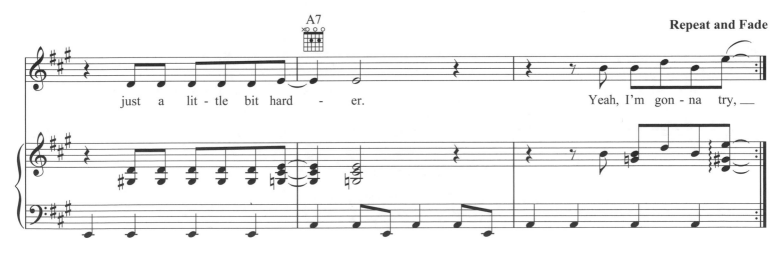

Additional Lyrics

2. Yeah, I'm gonna try, yeah
   Just a little bit harder
   So I can give, give, give you
   Ev'ry bit of my soul.

   Yeah, I'm gonna try, yeah
   Just a little bit harder
   So I can show, show, show you
   My love with no control.

   I've waited so long for someone so fine
   I ain't gonna lose my chance (No, I ain't gonna lose it)
   Ain't gonna lose my chance to make him mine, oh, mine.

   Yeah, I'm gonna try *(To Fade)*

LITTLE GIRL BLUE

Words by LORENZ HART
Music by RICHARD RODGERS

Spoken: "You know, I really dug Nina Simone."

"When Nina sang Little Girl Blue, you could feel her pain, her spirit, her presence, her soul of her entire being."

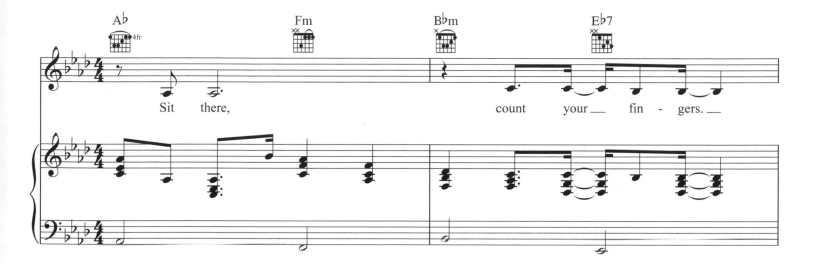

Sit there, count your __ fin - gers. __

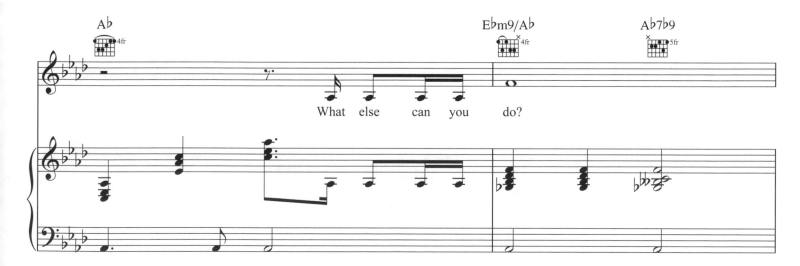

What else can you do?

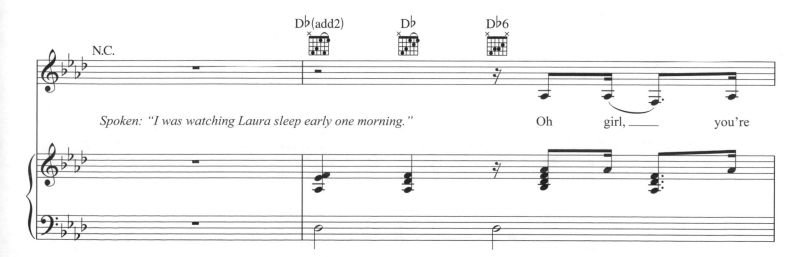

Spoken: "I was watching Laura sleep early one morning."

Oh girl, _____ you're

Spoken: "I could never sleep in those days, and I kept hearing Nina in my head."

through.

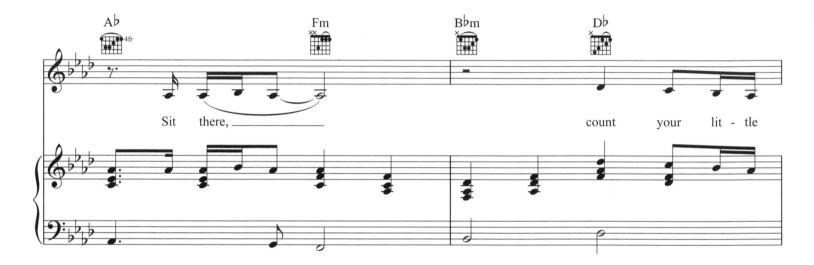

Sit there, _____ count your lit - tle

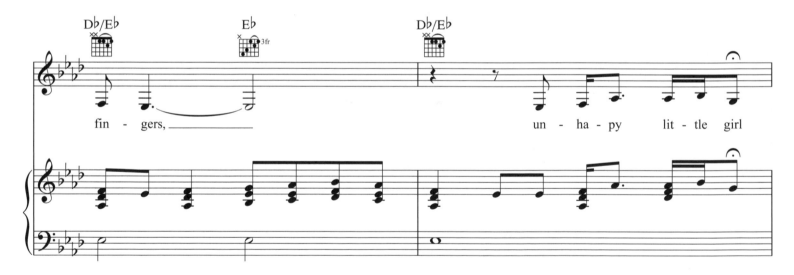

fin - gers, _____ un - ha - py lit - tle girl

blue. _____

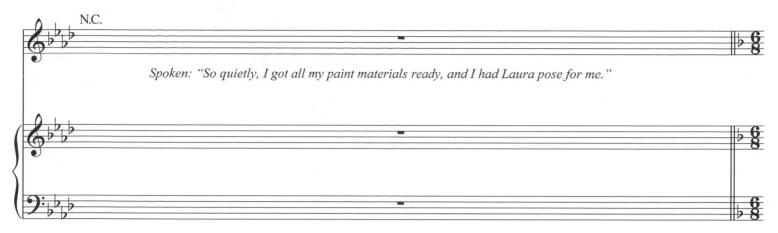

Spoken: "So quietly, I got all my paint materials ready, and I had Laura pose for me."

With movement

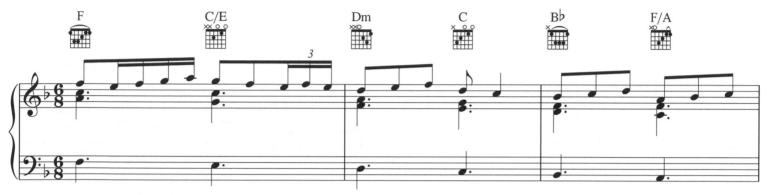

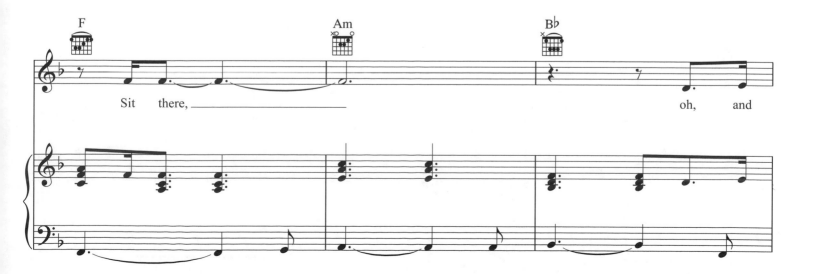

Sit there, _____ oh, and

count your fin - gers. _____ Hon-ey, what _ else, _____ what else _

_ can you do? _____ Hon - ey I

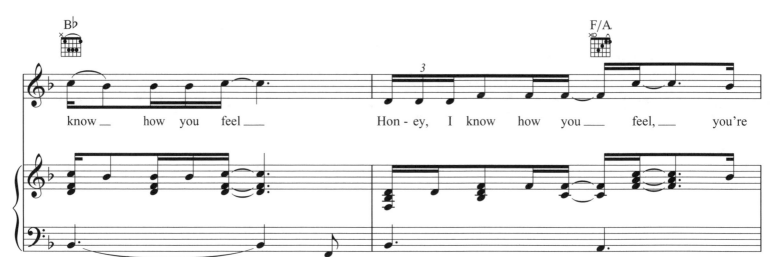

know _ how you feel _ Hon - ey, I know how you _ feel, _ you're

through. _____ Sit right back down. _

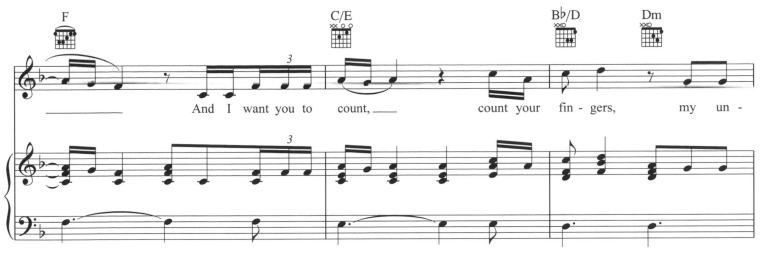

And I want you to count, ___ count your fin - gers, my un -

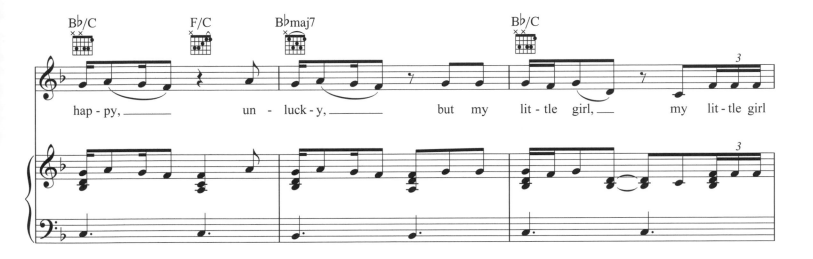

hap - py, ___ un - luck - y, ___ but my lit - tle girl, ___ my lit - tle girl

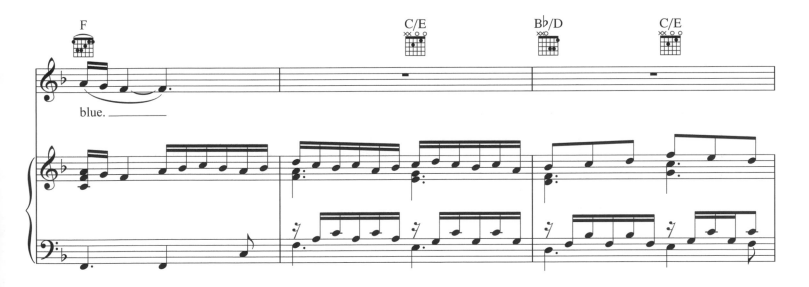

blue. ___

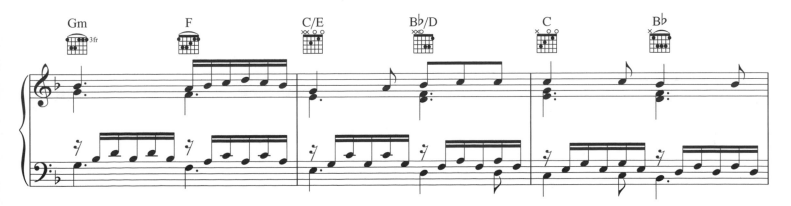

Well, sit there _____ to - day,

hon - ey, now go on, _____ want you to count those lit - tle rain - drops, _____

_____ I know they've been fall - ing down, _____

all a - round you, _____ and ev - 'ry - thing you have is gon - na work

out ___ on. An - y - thing you'll ev - er want to lean on, ev - 'ry - thing you're ev - er gon - na want to

lean, hon - ey, gon - na tell you right now, it's gon - na

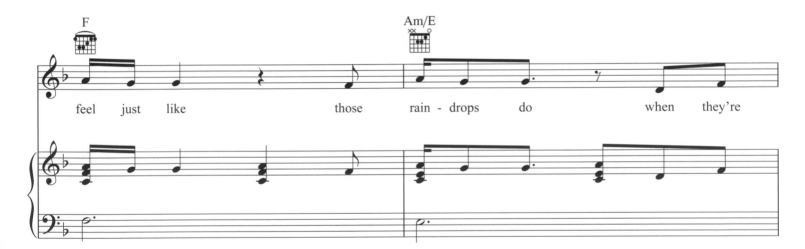

feel just like those rain - drops do when they're

fall - ing down, fall - ing all 'round, ___

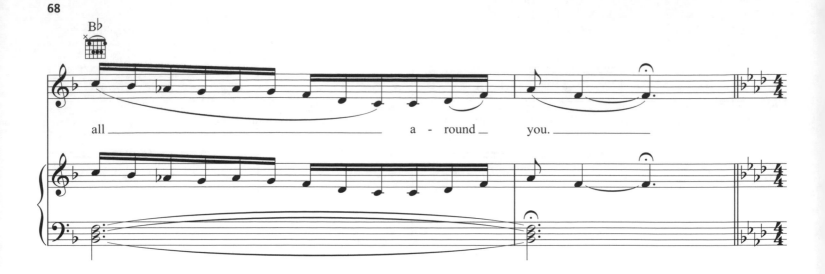

all _____ a - round ___ you. _____

With some freedom

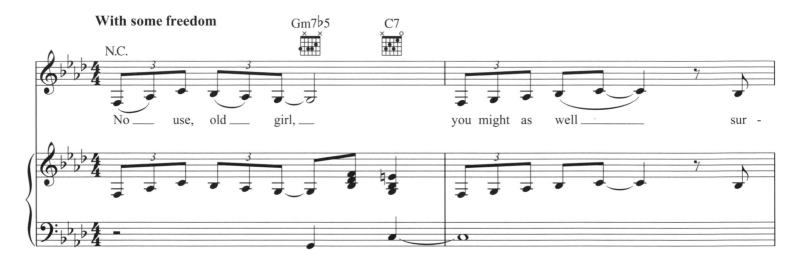

No ___ use, old ___ girl, ___ you might as well _____ sur -

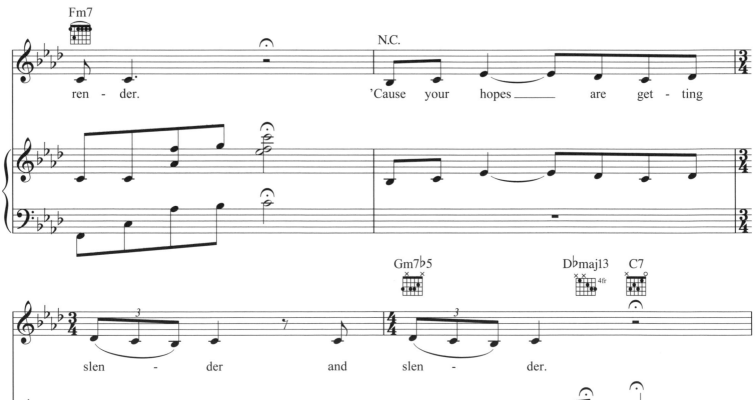

ren - der. 'Cause your hopes _____ are get - ting

slen - der and slen - der.

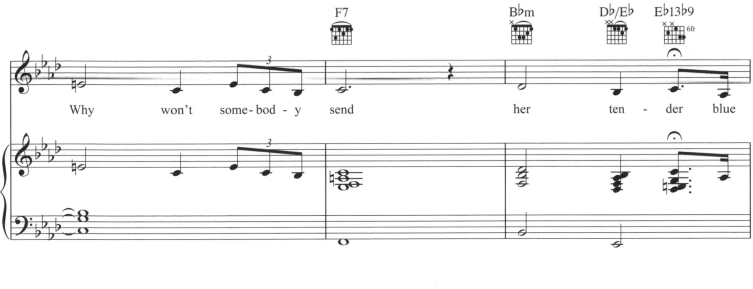

Why won't some-bod-y send her ten - der blue

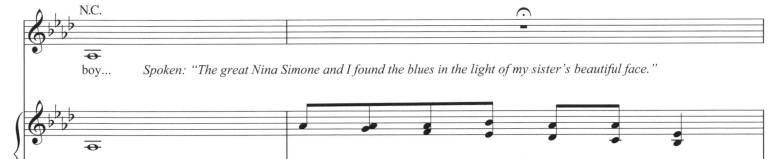

boy... *Spoken: "The great Nina Simone and I found the blues in the light of my sister's beautiful face."*

...to cheer up lit - tle girl blue. _____

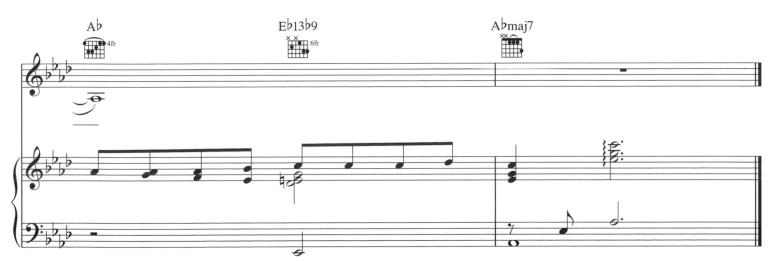

CRY BABY

Words and Music by NORMAN MEADE
and BERT RUSSELL

Moderately

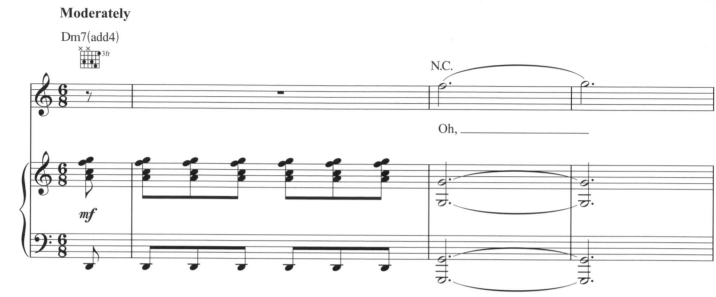

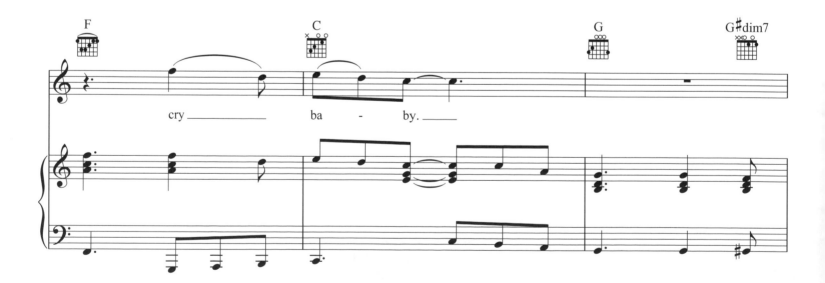

and cry,   cry,   ba - by. ____   Cry, ____

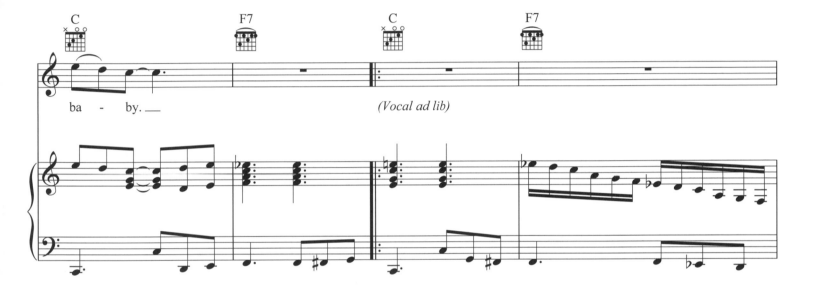

ba - by. ___   (Vocal ad lib)

Play 3 times

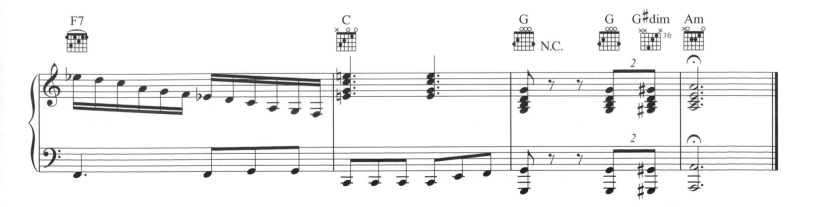

N.C.

KOZMIC BLUES

Words and Music by JANIS JOPLIN
and GABRIEL MEKLER

Slow Blues tempo

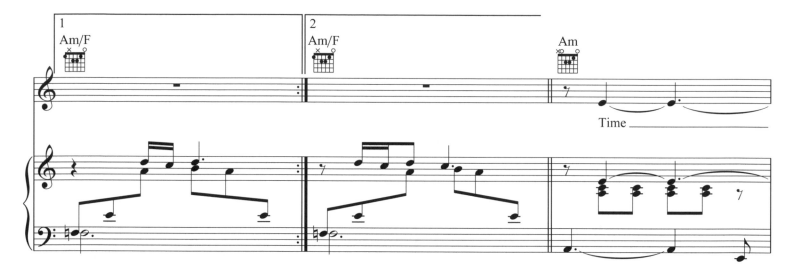

I keep mov- in' on, _____ but I nev-er found _____ out why. _ I keep

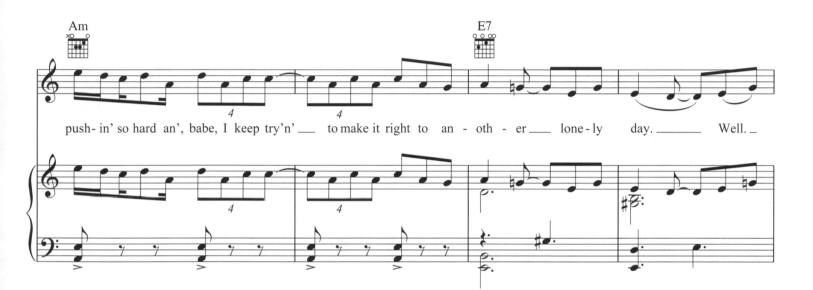

push- in' so hard an', babe, I keep try'n' ___ to make it right to an - oth - er ___ lone - ly day. _____ Well. _

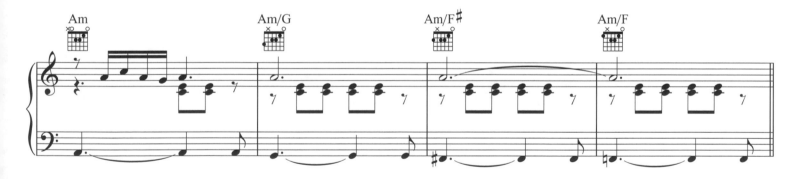

Dawn _____ has come at last, _____

Segue to "I Shall Be Released"

I SHALL BE RELEASED

Words and Music by
BOB DYLAN

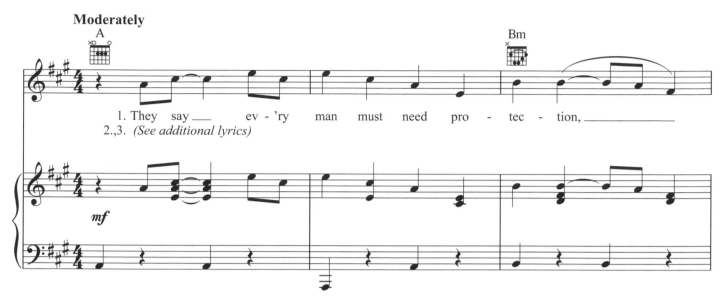

1. They say __ ev - 'ry man must need pro - tec - tion, __
2., 3. *(See additional lyrics)*

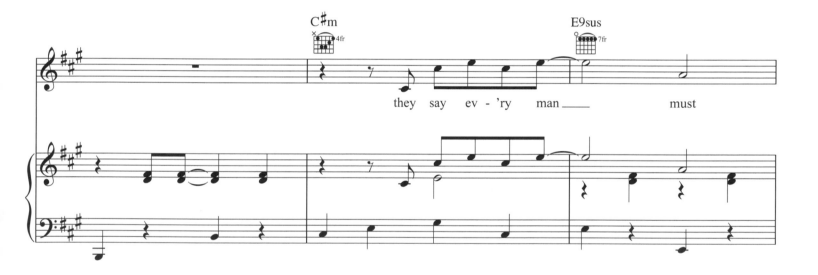

they say ev - 'ry man __ must

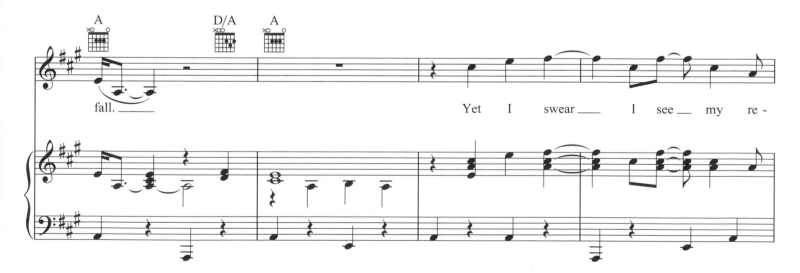

fall. __

Yet I swear __ I see my re-

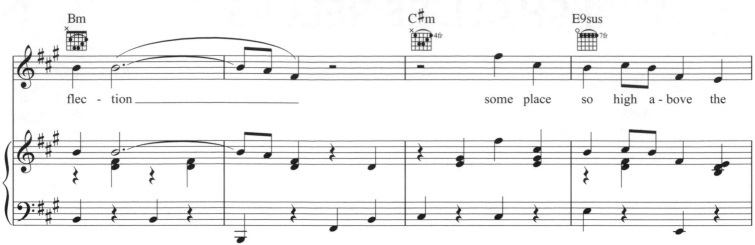

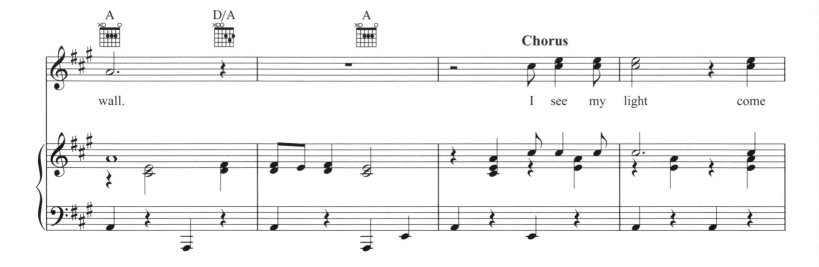

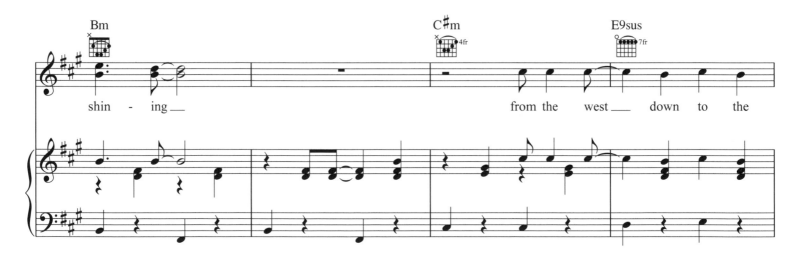

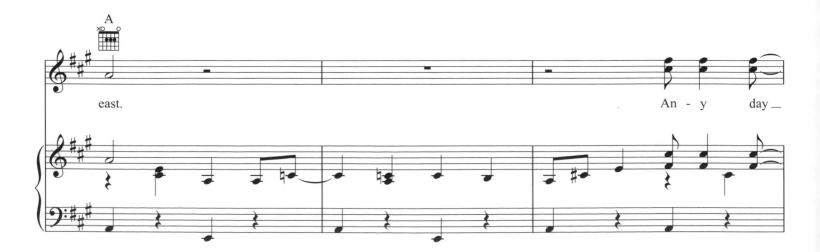

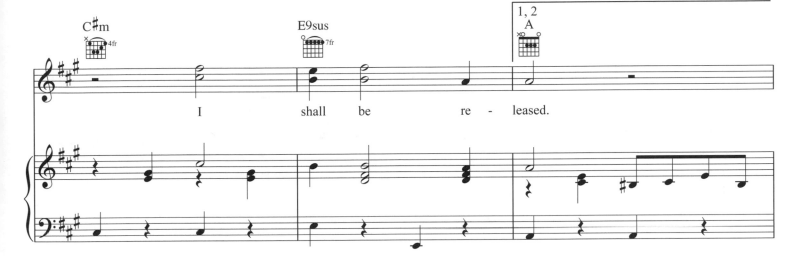

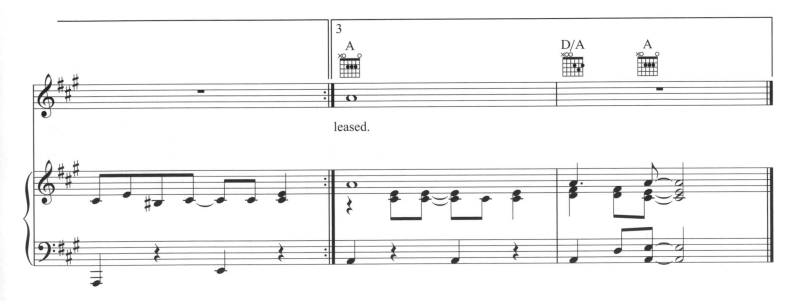

Additional Lyrics

2. Down here next to me in this lonely crowd
   Is a man who swears he's not to blame.
   All day long I hear him cry so loud,
   Calling out that he's been framed.
   Chorus

3. They say ev'rything can be replaced,
   Yet ev'ry distance is not near.
   So I remember ev'ry face
   Of ev'ry man who put me here.
   Chorus

ME AND BOBBY McGEE

Words and Music by KRIS KRISTOFFERSON
and FRED FOSTER

Busted flat in Baton Rouge, waitin' for a train, when I's feelin' near as faded as my jeans. Bobby thumbed a diesel down just before it rained. It rode us all the way into New Orleans. I

* *Vocal written one octave higher than sung.*

pulled my har-poon __ out of my dirt-y red __ ban-dan - a.　　　　I was

play - in' soft while Bob - by sang the blues, __ yeah. __

Wind - shield wip - ers slap - pin' time, __ I's __ hold - in' __ Bob-by's hand __ in mine;

we sang ev -'ry song __ that driv - er knew, __ yeah.　　　　Free-dom's just an-oth - er word　　for __

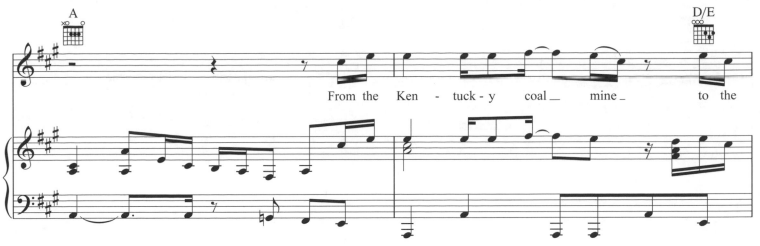

From the Ken - tuck - y coal __ mine __ to the

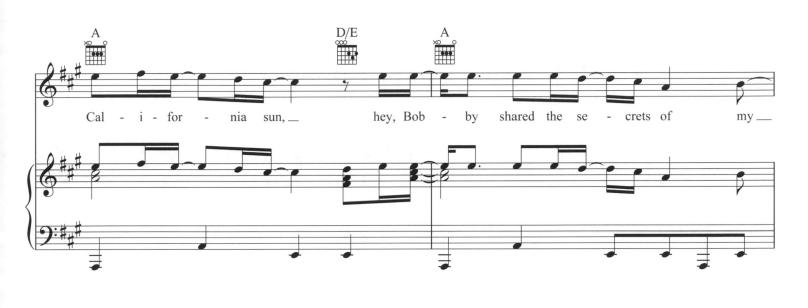

Cal - i - for - nia sun, __ hey, Bob - by shared the se - crets of my __

__ soul. Through all __ kinds of weath - er, through

ev - 'ry - thing __ we done, __ yeah, Bob - by ba - by kept me from the cold. __

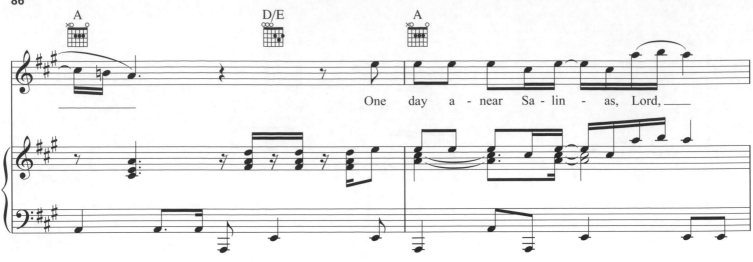

One day a - near Sa - lin - as, Lord,

I let him ___ slip a - way. ___ He's look - in' for that home ___ and I hope he

finds ___ it. ___ But I'd trade all of my to - mor - rows ___ for one

sin - gle ___ yes - ter - day ___ to be hold - in' Bob - by's bod - y next to mine. ___

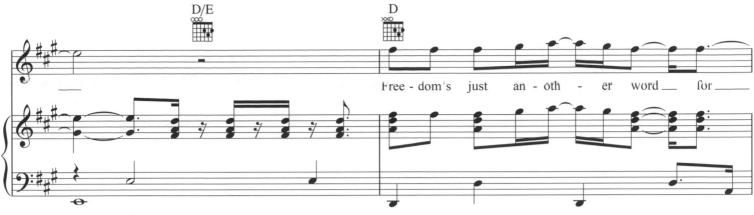

Free-dom's just an-oth-er word_ for_

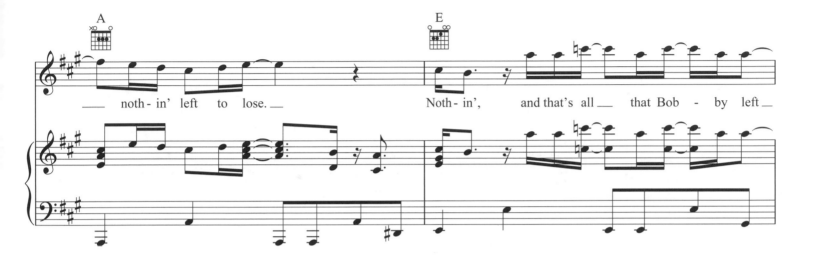

_ noth-in' left to lose. _ Noth-in', and that's all _ that Bob - by left _

_ me,_ yeah._ But if feel-in' good was eas - y, Lord,_

_ when he _ sang the blues, _ hey, feel-in' good was good e-nough_ for me,_

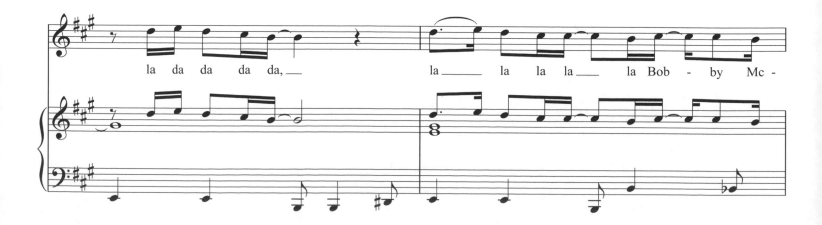

yeah. __ And then when I called __ him my lov - er, called him my man; __ I said I

called him my lov - er, did the best I can. __ Come on, hey now, Bob - by, now, hey now, Bob - by Mc - Gee, __

__ yeah. __ Lo la lo __ la lo __ la lo __ la lo __ la lo __

__ la lo __ la lo __ lo, ley, hey, hey, __ Bob - by Mc - Gee, __

Lord.

La la la____ la la____ la la____ la la____ la la____

____ la la____ la la,____ hey, hey, hey, Bob-by Mc - Gee,____ ah.

BALL AND CHAIN

Words and Music by
WILLIE MAE (BIG MAMA) THORNTON

(1.) Sit - tin' by my win - dow, and ___ I was look - in' out ___
(2.,4.) oh, oh, ba - by, why ___ you wan - na do these ___
(3.) *(Spoken:) I know you gonna miss me, baby, oh yes, you're gonna miss*

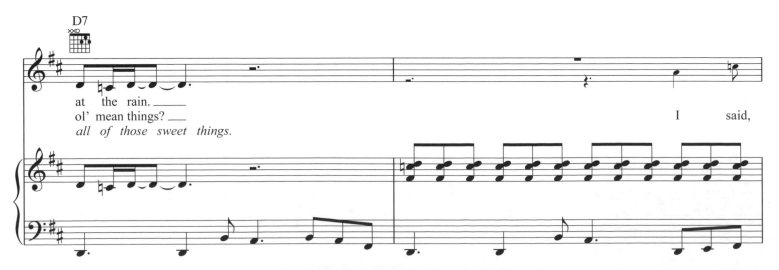

at the rain. ___
ol' mean things? ___ I said,
all of those sweet things.

Sit - tin' by my win - dow, ba - by,　and　I was sit - tin' there
oh,　oh,　ba - by,　why　you wan - na do these
I know you're gonna miss me, baby,　*you're gonna miss all of those*

look - in' out　at　the rain.
ol' mean things　to　me?
sweet,　sweet　things.

And then you'll find

You know　some - thin' struck me,
Be - cause　you know I love you,
that your whole life will be like mine,

clamped on　to　me　just
and I'm so sick　and
all wrapped up

STAY WITH ME

Words and Music by JERRY RAGOVOY
and GEORGE DAVID WEISS

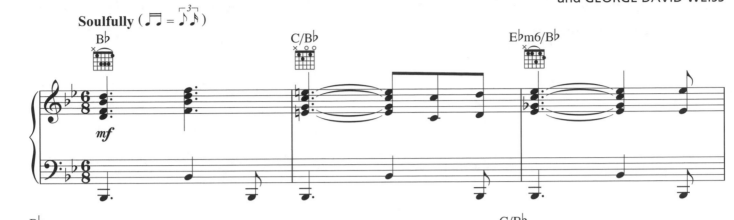

care of you? _____ But look out, can't be-lieve you're ev - er gon - na leave.

Stay _____ with me, ba - by. Stay _____ with me,

ba - by. Stay _____ with me, ba - by. Oh, hon - ey, won't you

stay? Won't you stay, ba - by.

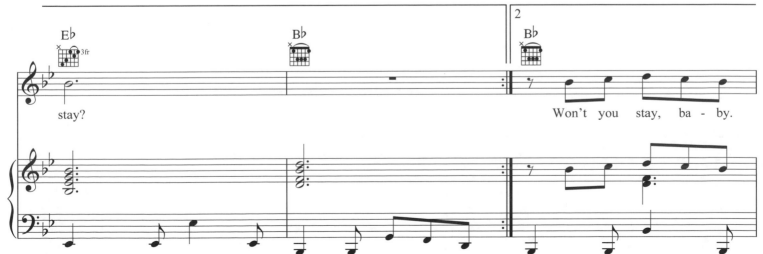

ba - by, hey._____ Stay _____ with me

ba - by. Stay _____ with me ba - by.

Won't you stay, ba - by. Hon - ey, come on, won't you stay 'cause you know that, you know that I
Won't you stay, ba - by. Won't you stay,__ ba - by, I

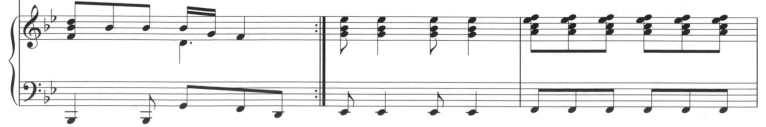

just can't go on._____ can't go, can't go...

Stay _____ with me, ba - by, ba - by, ba - by. I'm

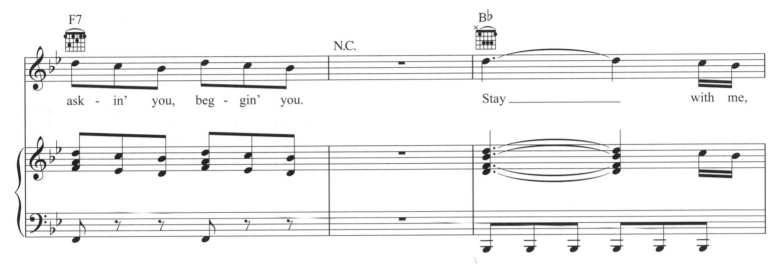

ask - in' you, beg - gin' you. Stay _____ with me,

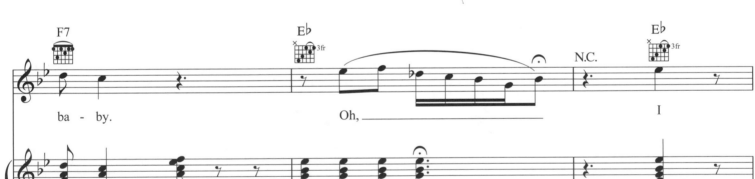

ba - by. Oh, _____ I

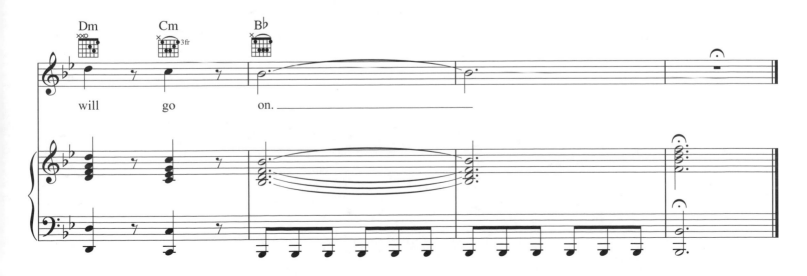

will go on. _____

I'M GONNA ROCK MY WAY TO HEAVEN

Words and Music by JERRY RAGOVOY
and JENNI DEAN

Rock 'n' Roll

No mat-ter where __ I

go from here, __ at least I know __ I had ___ my say. __ There's

some - thing ___ I'm gon-na tell ___ you right ___ now, I tell you it's the on - ly ___

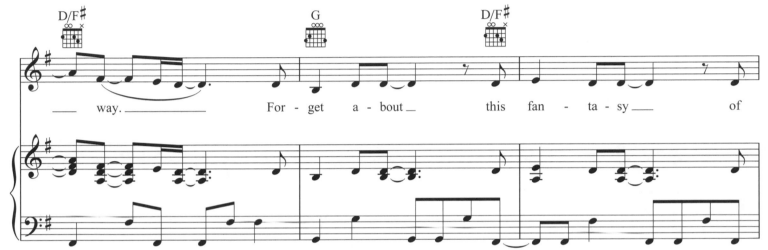

___ way. _____ For - get a - bout ___ this fan - ta - sy ___ of

jus - tice, where's ___ the truth? _____ Now, they'll say it's day ___ when you know ___

___ damn well ___ it's night. Don't waste it on you. _____

Get your-self __ to-geth - er in-side. __ I'm nev - er far, now you know why __

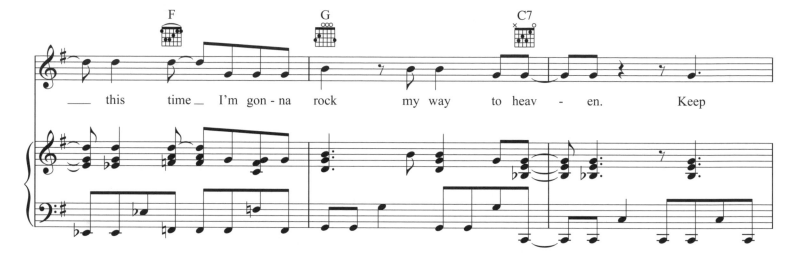

__ this time __ I'm gon - na rock my way to heav - en. Keep

rock - ing my way to heav - en. I'm gon - na rock my way to heav-

- en, oh _____ yes I ___ am. _____

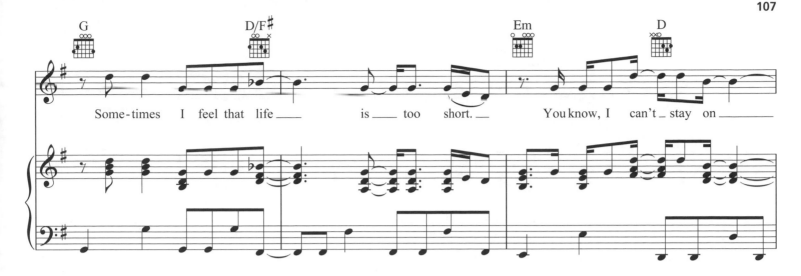

Some-times I feel that life ___ is ___ too short. ___ You know, I can't ___ stay on ___

___ the run. ___ And I'm ___ nev - er, I'm nev-er look-ing back, ___ I'm gon-na

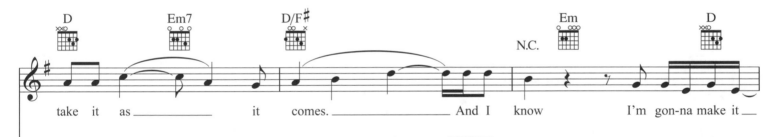

take it as _____ it comes. _____ And I know I'm gon-na make it ___

___ this time, ___ 'cause it's been ___ my time. Weight is off ___ my mind. ___

Rock my way to heav - en. Keep rock-ing my way to heav-

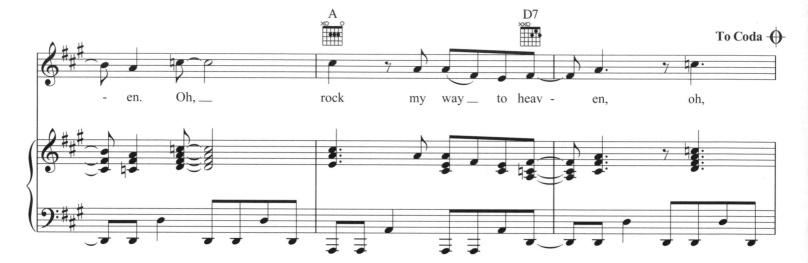

- en. Oh, rock my way to heav - en, oh,

yes I am. yes I am.

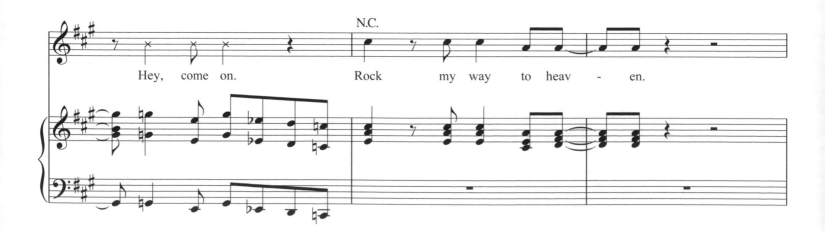

Hey, come on. Rock my way to heav - en.

Rock-ing my way to heav - en, Rock my way to heav -

D.S. al Coda

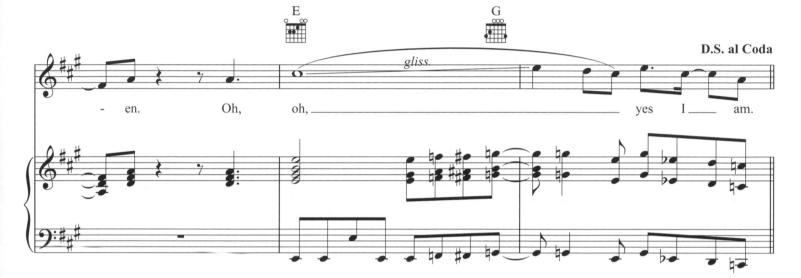

- en. Oh, oh, _____ yes I ___ am.

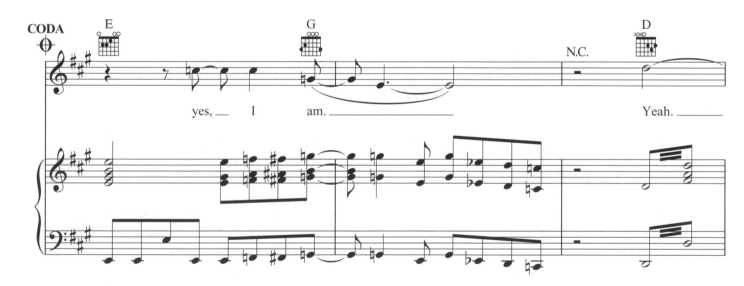

CODA yes, ___ I am. _____ Yeah. _____

___ Yeah. Yeah. _____

MERCEDES BENZ

Words and Music by JANIS JOPLIN,
MICHAEL McCLURE and BOB NEUWIRTH

(Spoken:) I'd like to do a song of great social and political import.
It goes like this:

In a moderate, hand-clapping 2

Fine

(Spoken:) That's it!

Mer - ce - des Benz? Oh, Lord, won't you buy me _____ a

col - or T. V.? ___ Dial - ing for Dol - lars is try - ing to find me. __

___ I wait for de - liv - er - y each day un - til

three. _____ So, Lord, _____ won't you buy me ___ a col - or T. -

112